A Maple Spring
Sugar Season In Northern Michigan

First Edition 2011
Revised Edition 2015

Rozanski, W. Scott.
A Maple Spring, Sugar Season In Northern Michigan / Scott W. Rozanski ;
Illustrated photos by Scott W. Rozanski – 2nd ed.

Summary: This book is about making maple syrup in northern Michigan. It was
created for children and instruction.

The book was typeset in Century Schoolbook.

Illustrations are actual digital photos of our family and our maple syrup
production. The pictures were then enhanced by software to appear oil based.

A Maple Spring
Sugar Season In Northern Michigan

Written by Scott Rozanski

After a long cold winter, which is common across northern Michigan, spring is a welcome time of year. Spring is a transition period, from months of snow blowing the driveway and blinding lake effect snow off Lake Michigan, to warmer days and melting snow. It is a time to get outdoors, smell the fresh cool snow melt air and soak up the sun. Most importantly, it is a time to begin making maple syrup.

We have been making our own maple syrup in the forests of northern Michigan since 2001. During our first maple syrup season, our children were young, Tyler was 7 and Abbey was 5. My wife and I home schooled our children and making syrup was part of their education.

Our maple syrup operation has changed over the years, but the basic idea has stayed the same. Tap the trees, collect the sap, boil the sap and bottle the final product. On average we make between three and five gallons of maple syrup each season. Our best year was in 2003 when we made a total of eleven gallons.

Our children are much older now. Their lives have become busier as you would expect, but we still enjoy making maple syrup. I hope you enjoy spending some time with us during our Maple Spring, Sugar Season In Northern Michigan.

Northern Michigan is unique in many ways; the Great Lakes, the Mackinac Bridge and four distinct seasons. Northern Michigan is also unique by its position on the globe. The 45th Parallel intersects the region generally between Traverse City and Alpena. This makes northern Michigan half way between the North Pole and the Equator.

Northern Michigan has another aspect which makes it unique, it is home to an abundance of sugar maple trees. These trees are used each spring to harvest pure maple syrup. A stand of sugar maple trees, to maple syrup producers, is known as a sugar bush. Sugar maples are also called hard maple or rock maple, and are often used to make furniture.

Sugar maple trees are considered a hard wood or deciduous tree, meaning they lose their leaves each Autumn. During winter months these trees are dormant in the deep snow of the long northern Michigan winters. The only sign of life during this time is when the trees sway and creek during the frequent north winds.

Just when it seems the cold and gray stare of winter will continue without end, the first hints of spring arrive in late February. Rings begin to form around the base of the trees as a warmer sun rides higher in the southern sky. I refer to these rings as sugar rings, because I know sugar season is near.

Once the sugar rings form and the first drips of melting ice and snow are seen falling from rooftops, preparations for the maple syrup season begins. Drill bits, spiles, filters, sap buckets and boiling pans are gathered and inspected.

Tapping trees is the first step. Originally a hand tool known as the brace and bit was used to drill holes into the trees. With the onset of improved battery technology, 18 volt cordless drills have become more commonly used.

A 7/16 inch bore bit is used to drill a hole about 1 ½ inches into the tree. The hole is drilled at a slight angle to help the flow of sap, and is usually drilled about 4 feet above the ground. Tapping is done on the south side of the tree, where the sun warms the trunk early in the day, helping sap run quickly.

Tyler uses the 18 volt cordless drill, which increases the amounts of taps that can be completed during the day.

The most productive place to tap a tree, is between a main root and large limb in the above canopy. Sap is a sugar water liquid which flows from the roots to the branches above, and is food for the leaves. Sap flows just inside the bark and is clear just like water. Try some sap and see for yourself.

The hole should be cleaned, using a small flat head screw driver or small paint can pry bar. This helps to remove any lingering wood shavings. Then a spile is inserted into the hole and tapped lightly with a hammer to set it in place.

Sap seems to flow best on sunny days with afternoon temperatures in the 40s, and nighttime lows in the 20s.

Finally a sap collector is placed on the spile to catch sap when it begins to flow. Most anything can be used. Galvanized buckets, plastic pales, one gallon milk jugs and plastic bags are commonly used. It is important to remember, that when smaller collectors are used, you may need to empty more often once the sap begins to flow.

We enjoy using the larger blue sap bags and bag holders. The bag holder helps keep rain and bark from getting into the sap. Tyler assembles the sap bag before hanging it on the spile.

The work is not done yet, a good supply of wood is very important for maple syrup production. Tyler usually cuts and splits between one and two face cord depending on how much syrup we plan to make. A face cord is 4 foot high, 8 foot long with chucks of wood 16 to 20 inches long. Dry hard wood is the most efficient at producing heat and creating hot coals, which is needed to boil sap into maple syrup.

Our fuzzy dog Touke (as in tuque the stocking hat worn in Canada), is a fairly typical Golden Retriever. She enjoys being involved in all aspects of our lives, including the maple syrup season. As you can see, she is very helpful.

Once the sap begins to flow, its needs to be collected and stored until it can be processed into maple syrup. We store our sap in large 33 gallon drums. When enough sap has been collected it is time to begin the boiling process. In order to make syrup from sap, the water needs to be separated from the sugar. This is done by boiling the sap. Water rises from the sap in the form of steam. Large pots or pans are used to boil the sap.

To being the boiling process we place the pan on two rows of cement block. The blocks are stacked three rows high, to allow enough room under the pan to create a hot fire.

The pan we use is large, but shallow and crafted from stainless steel. It is 4 feet long, 22 inches wide and 3 inches deep. This pan has a large surface area which allows for the rapid removal of water from the sap. Quickly removing the water from the sap reduces the amount of boil time and usually produces a lighter colored syrup.

Before the first run of the season we test the equipment. Abbey starts a small fire and melts snow in the pan. The liquid is then drained off through the spigot, to make sure everything is working properly.

Sap is then added to the pan and the boiling process begins. We are careful not to overflow the pan because the sap can boil vigorously and splash out. As the steam begins to rise, the liquid level in the pan lowers, so more sap is added. We usually pre-heat sap in a smaller pan before adding it to the larger pan, so we do not lose the boil and slow the evaporation process.

When we add additional sap we are careful, so we do not overfill the pan. We count the number of gallons added to each patch, so we can calculate a sap to syrup ratio.

Sap is considered maple syrup once the liquid boils to between 7 and 9 degrees above the boiling point. At these temperatures most of the water is released as steam leaving a higher concentration of sugar, known as maple syrup.

The boiling point of sap, even though mostly water, does not necessarily boil at 212 degrees. The boiling point is dependent on atmospheric pressure and can vary daily. Generally the boiling point of sap in northern Michigan is between 209 and 211 degrees. Its important to take a temperature reading of the sap as soon as it begins to boil. We use a digital cooking thermometer.

Since sap is mainly water with only a small part sugar, the ratio of sap to syrup is generally very high. At the beginning of the season when sap has the highest sugar content, it usually takes 30 to 40 gallons of sap to make one gallon of maple syrup. Toward the end of the season, the ratio increases to around 70 gallons of sap to one gallon of maple syrup.

When boiling sap, a skim forms on top of the liquid which Abbey removes to keep the liquid clear. At the beginning stages, sap boils large and clear just like water. Toward the end of the process and closer to true maple syrup, the number of bubbles increase and become much smaller. The bubbles become more golden in color and begins to smell sweet.

Once the temperature of the boiling sap increases to seven degrees above the boiling point of the day, we drain the liquid from the pan. Remember, each boiling day is different and sap does not always start boiling at 212 degrees. Depending on atmospheric pressure and sugar content, the sap will actually initially boil at a temperatures lower than 212 degrees.

When we drain the pan, we run the hot liquid through a felt filter. Running the syrup through this felt removes any debris that collected during the boiling process; such as ash from the fire or bark from the trees.

The liquid is then placed into a smaller pot to increase the temperature by one more degree completing the final boiling process. We use the smaller pot and smaller fires, for a more controlled boil. The final product is pure maple syrup, made from your own backyard.

Kim watches the fire closely, adding only small amounts of wood. A large fire at this stage could make the syrup quickly overflow the pot.

After the syrup has been removed from the pan and filtered, we place snow into the pan and boil it down. Then we clean the pan and remove it from the hot fire. Now we are all set for another day of boiling sap into maple syrup.

Maple syrup, bottled and ready for breakfast the next morning.

Making maple syrup is hard work, with long hours. However the reward of spending "A Maple Spring, Sugar Season In Northern Michigan" is worth it.

Enjoy what nature provided and you created.

We hope you enjoyed spending some time with us as we made homemade maple syrup, and that you learned enough to make your own maple syrup. Soon the winds will change and snow will once again cover the northern Michigan landscape. But as always, in late February and early March the sun will begin warming the trees and sugar rings will appear...signifying that it is time for another "Maple Spring, Sugar Season In Northern Michigan." Until then....